D0771204

D.I.Y. MAKE IT HAPPEN

BABYSITTERS' CLUB

VIRGINIA LOH-HAGAN

Camas Public Library

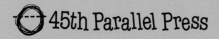
45th Parallel Press

Published in the United States of America by Cherry Lake Publishing
Ann Arbor, Michigan
www.cherrylakepublishing.com

Reading Adviser: Marla Conn, ReadAbility, Inc.
Book Designer: Felicia Macheske

Photo Credits: © yzoa/Shutterstock.com, cover, 1, 10; © ziashusha/Shutterstock.com, 3; © Huntstock.com/Shutterstock.com, 5; © lendy16/Shutterstock.com, 7; © DAJ/Thinkstock, 9; © dragon_fang/Shutterstock.com, 11; © Iaremenko Sergii/Shutterstock.com, 12; © Halfpoint/Shutterstock.com, 15; © OksanaAriskina/Shutterstock.com, 16; © Deborah Kolb/Shutterstock.com, 18; © Bloomua/Shutterstock.com, 19; © bikeriderlondon/Shutterstock.com, 21; © Lucky Business/Shutterstock.com, 23; © Jaimie Duplass/Shutterstock.com, 24; © aopsan/Shutterstock.com, 25; © deamles for sale/Tania Zbrodko/Shutterstock.com, 27; © Sergey Novikov/Shutterstock.com, 28; © Valentina Razumova/Shutterstock.com, 29; © Drinevskaya Olga/Shutterstock.com, 31; © wavebreakmedia/Shutterstock.com, back cover; © Dora Zett/Shutterstock.com, back cover

Graphic Elements: © pashabo/Shutterstock.com, 6, back cover; © axako/Shutterstock.com, 7; © IreneArt/Shutterstock.com, 4, 8; © bokasin/Shutterstock.com, 11, 19; © topform/Shutterstock.com, 11, 19, back cover; © Belausava Volha/Shutterstock.com, 12, 24; © Nik Merkulov/Shutterstock.com, 13; © Ya Tshey/Shutterstock.com, 14, 27; © Art'nLera/Shutterstock.com, 14, back cover; © kubais/Shutterstock.com, 16; © Sasha Nazim/Shutterstock.com, 17, 20; © Ursa Major/Shutterstock.com, 23, 28; © Infomages/Shutterstock.com, 26

Copyright © 2016 by Cherry Lake Publishing
All rights reserved. No part of this book may be reproduced or utilized in any form or by any means without written permission from the publisher.

45th Parallel Press is an imprint of Cherry Lake Publishing.

Library of Congress Cataloging-in-Publication Data

Loh-Hagan, Virginia, author.
  Babysitters club / by Virginia Loh-Hagan.
    pages cm. — (D.I.Y. make it happen)
  Includes bibliographic references and index.
  ISBN 978-1-63470-496-0 (hardcover) — ISBN 978-1-63470-556-1 (pdf) — ISBN 978-1-63470-616-2 (pbk.) — ISBN 978-1-63470-676-6 (ebook)
  1. Babysitting—Juvenile literature. I. Title.
  HQ769.5.L64 2015
  649'.1—dc23
                    2015026841

Cherry Lake Publishing would like to acknowledge the work of The Partnership for 21st Century Skills.
Please visit www.p21.org for more information.

Printed in the United States of America
Corporate Graphics Inc.

ABOUT THE AUTHOR

Dr. Virginia Loh-Hagan is an author, university professor, former classroom teacher, and curriculum designer. Her first job was babysitting. Babysitting was the main way she made money in college. She lives in San Diego with her very tall husband and very naughty dogs. To learn more about her, visit www.virginialoh.com.

TABLE OF CONTENTS

CHAPTER ONE

WHAT DOES IT MEAN TO START A BABYSITTERS' CLUB?

Do you love children? Do you love planning? Do you love leading? Then starting a babysitters' club is the right project for you!

Babysitters care for children. They do it for a short time. They do it for hours. They work different hours. They work different days. They babysit when needed.

A babysitters' club is a group. It's a group of babysitters. They join together. They help each other. They share **clients**. Clients are people who hire babysitters.

Talk to other babysitters.
Get their opinions.

KNOW THE LINGO

Au pair: a babysitter from another country who lives with a host family

Charge: the child a babysitter takes care of

CPR: cardiopulmonary resuscitation, a lifesaving technique to help people who aren't breathing

Infant: a baby, babies can't walk yet

Live-in nanny: someone who lives with their charges; their pay includes room and board

LO: little one, used when talking online about children so as to protect their identities

Manny: a male nanny

Mother's helper: someone who babysits and helps the mother with chores

Nanny family: the family that employs the nanny (a full-time babysitter)

Newborn: a baby who has just been born

Night nanny: a babysitter who watches a child overnight

Toddler: a child between the ages of one and three; a walking child

Start a babysitters' club whenever you want. Babysitters are in demand. They're needed all the time!

Parents leave the house. They work. They run errands. They hang out with other adults. They need help. They hire a babysitter. The babysitter cares for their children. One babysitter can't help them all. A babysitters' club gives parents more choices.

Some babysitters work for experience. They want to work with children. Many babysitters do it to make money. Babysitters can make about $10 an hour. Starting a babysitters' club is a good idea. You can make more money. You'll meet new people. You'll learn new skills. You'll also have fun!

Check the going rate for babysitting. Ask parents what they pay. Ask other babysitters what they charge.

CHAPTER TWO

WHAT DO YOU NEED TO START A BABYSITTERS' CLUB?

A club needs members. Get members. Gather other babysitters. Gather friends.

➡ Ask if they've babysat before. You want people who have cared for children.

➡ Check **references**. A reference is a good review. This means clients like the service.

➡ Do a **background check**. Ask around. Make sure they haven't been in trouble.

Decide roles.

➡ The **president** is the leader. She plans meetings. She talks to clients. She assigns babysitting jobs.

➡ The **vice president** helps the president. She's in charge of training.

➡ The **treasurer** takes care of money.

➡ The **secretary** takes care of paperwork. She helps schedule.

Make sure you have a phone the club can use.

Learn about your members. Know what they can do. Know what your club can offer.

➡ Decide who your members can babysit. Some members care for babies. Some care for young children.

➡ Decide when members can babysit. Some can work after school. Some can work on weekends. Some can work at night. Some can work during school breaks.

➡ Keep track of members' skills. Keep track of their experiences.

Think of a club name. This is how you'll be known.

➡ Come up with several names. Your name should be fun. Relate it to kids.

➡ Discuss the top choices.

➡ Choose the best name. All members should agree.

Babysitter For

HIRE!

Bubbly
Attentive
Beautiful

Make sure you can tell clients about your club members' skills.

Your club needs rules.

➡ **Decide when you want to meet. Once a week? Once a month?**

➡ **Decide your meeting place. Use what's available. Meet at a member's home or the library.**

➡ **Decide how you'll work together.**

A club shares jobs. Members get more money. More families get help.

➡ **Make a list of clients.**

➡ **Create a Web site. Share contact information. Share good comments. Explain how you help parents.**

➡ **Create business cards. Include your club name. Include the president's first name. Include the phone number.**

➡ **Create posters. Put them where parents go. An example is a grocery store.**

Your club name goes here.

Be safe. Don't include your whole name. Don't share personal information.

TRY THIS!

The Baby-Sitters Club is a series of books. It's written by Ann M. Martin. There are over 130 books. There are more books in spin-off series. Spin-offs are books inspired by the original. Form a book club with your babysitters' club. Pick one book from the series. Make sure each member of your club has a copy.

You'll need: *The Baby-Sitters Club* books, snacks

Steps

1 Pick a date to discuss the book. Pick a place.

2 Read the book.

3 Host a book club discussion. Provide snacks.

4 Discuss what you liked about the book. Discuss what you didn't like.

5 Make connections to your babysitting jobs.

6 Make connections to your babysitters' club.

7 Discuss how you would solve the problems presented in the books.

8 Write down your stories.

CHAPTER THREE

HOW DO YOU SET UP A BABYSITTERS' CLUB?

Develop a plan for paying.

- Decide your fees. A fee is how much you'll charge. Most babysitters charge per hour. Some charge extra. They charge per child. Some clients provide rides. Clubs charge them less.

- Have members pay dues. Dues are club fees. The club buys things. Dues pay for them. Decide the cost of dues.

- Open a bank account. Have the treasurer do this.

Develop a scheduling plan. Get a calendar.

➡ **Clients call the president. The president learns what clients need. (How many hours? When?)**

➡ **The president works with the secretary. The secretary has everyone's schedule. The president assigns jobs to members.**

➡ **The president calls clients back. Do it right away.**

Keep the costs the same.
Everyone should know your rates.

SHEILA LIRIO MARCELO

Sheila Lirio Marcelo is a Filipino American. She's a chief executive officer. Her company is like a huge babysitting club. It's called Care.com. It connects clients to babysitters. The company does background checks. It provides references. She needed help finding child care for her own kids. That inspired her to start Care.com. She said, "At some point, every person needs help with care." She wants to help families. She wants people to work and raise families. She wants people to know their kids are well cared for. Starting a babysitters' club is like starting a small business. She said, "It will be scary and exhilarating and at times not at all what you expected. But if you're following your passion, it will also be one of the greatest things you ever do."

Talk to parents. Discuss discipline, food and eating habits, bedtime routines, and house rules.

Have the secretary call new clients. Learn about them. Get information. More details are better.

➡ **Find out how many children they have.**

➡ **Find out where they live.**

➡ **Make a collection of cards. Each card has client information. Include phone numbers. Include medical information. Include interests. Members should take this to jobs. Only share these cards with club members.**

The vice president organizes training. Members need training. Many local places provide classes. Clients like having trained babysitters.

➡ **Get first aid training. Children fall. They get hurt. First aid helps them.**

➡ **Get emergency training. An emergency is when something dangerous happens. An example is choking. No one expects it. But babysitters should be prepared.**

Have each member fill out a report. Do this for each job. Keep reports for club records.

➡ **Describe what you did.**

➡ **Describe what went well.**

➡ **Describe what you'll work on next time.**

➡ **Share with clients.**

Thank clients after each job.

➡ **Have the secretary call the clients. Ask about the service. Ask what they liked. Ask what the club can improve.**

➡ **Ask them to give nice comments for your Web site.**

➡ **Ask them to recommend your club. They tell other people. They promote your club.**

➡ **Offer rewards. Offer free child care. Give clients a free hour after 10 jobs. Give them a free hour for new clients they recommend.**

Create forms to keep track of each client, babysitter, and job.

CHAPTER FOUR

HOW DO YOU RUN A BABYSITTERS' CLUB MEETING?

You've got members. You've got jobs. You're ready to host club meetings!

First, the president creates an **agenda**. This is a meeting schedule. It lists goals. It lists talking points.

➡ Include a treasurer's report. Tell members how much money was made. Tell them how much money was spent.

➡ Include a secretary's report. Tell members about new club members. Tell them about new clients.

➡ Include time for club members to share. They can solve problems.

➡ **Include time to do activities.**

➡ **Include time to learn something new.**

Before the meeting, send the agenda to all your members.

Make sure members are comfortable.

➡ **Provide chairs for everyone.**

➡ **Provide drinks and snacks. Or host a potluck. Each person brings food. Everyone shares.**

➡ **Provide time to hang out.**

➡ **Ask members to share good news.**

The president leads meetings. The secretary takes notes. Notes are called minutes.

➡ **Call the meeting to order. Start the meeting.**

➡ **Take roll call. Call members' names. Note who's there. Note who's not there.**

➡ **Make sure everyone agrees with the agenda. You can change the order. You can add new items.**

➡ **Remind everyone to take turns speaking.**

➡ **Go through the agenda items.**

Consider recording your meetings.

Meetings can be fun. Have members do things together. They can help the club. They can create kits. These kits are for jobs. They're things to do with children. They're called kid-kits.

➡ **Include first aid items. These should be in all kits. Put in Band-Aids. Put in cleaning wipes. Put in healing cream.**

➡ **Create a games kit. Put in playing cards. Put in puzzles. Put in board games.**

➡ **Create a reading kit. Put in several books. Put in several magazines. Consider the children's ages.**

➡ **Create an art kit. Put in paper. Put in coloring books. Put in drawing tools.**

➡ **Create project kits. Think of fun projects. Bring all the tools you need. Work with children to do the projects.**

Use tote bags that can be zipped up.

QUICK TIPS

- Discuss how to deal with separation anxiety. Some kids get upset about leaving their parents. They may cry. They may throw fits. Brainstorm ways to distract them.

- Tell your club members to not wear dangling jewelry. Young children like to pull on these things.

- Recruit the right people. Noa Mintz started her own babysitting club. She was 12 years old. It became a company. It's called Nannies by Noa. She has more than 200 clients. She needed to finish high school. She hired a person to be in charge. She's making lots of money.

- Tell your club members to practice babysitting. Have them babysit family members. Have them babysit neighbors' kids.

- Sometimes, your club members will be babysitting for people they don't know. Make sure everyone stays safe. Know where your club members are.

- Contact former clients. Let them know you'd love to see their kids. Let them know your club is available.

Have members learn something new.

➡ **Teach them new games. An example is a favorite toy hunt. The babysitter asks children to get their favorite toys. The babysitter hides them. The children find them.**

➡ **Teach them tips to deal with fits. An example is talking things out. The babysitter asks the child to state the problem. They discuss solutions. Practice talking calmly.**

➡ **Teach them cooking ideas. An example is bagel face. The babysitter spreads cream cheese on a bagel. Children add fruit pieces. They add vegetable pieces. They make a face.**

➡ **Teach them cleaning tips. An example is vinegar. Vinegar can help get out ketchup stains. Apply vinegar. Then put the item in the wash.**

Learn and share ways to keep children happy and busy.

Adjourning, or ending, the meeting means the business is over. But club members can still hang out.

The president ends the meeting.

- ➡ **Ask for comments. Ask for questions.**
- ➡ **Set the next meeting date.**
- ➡ **Review tasks that need to be done. Set deadlines.**
- ➡ **Thank everyone for coming.**
- ➡ **Have the secretary send minutes to all members.**

A babysitters' club is great for learning business skills. Club members support each other. They share tips. They share challenges. Starting a babysitters' club is a lot of work. But it's also a lot of fun. You get to hang out with friends. You get to make some money. You get to help your community.

D.I.Y. EXAMPLE!

STEPS	EXAMPLES
Get members	• Ask friends if they want to join your babysitting club. • Put up posters at school and libraries. • Have members submit skills and experiences.
Name	Club Care
Services	• Child care for children ages 3 to 8. • Child care on weekends and summers.
Dees and charges	• Club dues: $10 a month • Charges: $12 an hour • Free hour for every 10 jobs
Agenda for meeting	• Call meeting to order • Roll call • Approve agenda • Treasurer's and secretary's reports • Members share news and challenges • Vice president's training • Kid-kit creation

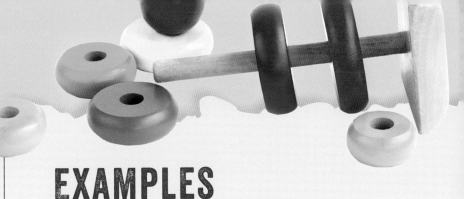

STEPS	EXAMPLES
Make a kid-kit	Make a project kit. Have children make their own jellyfish.

Make a project kit. Have children make their own jellyfish.

- Kid-kit should have: book about jellyfish, 2-liter bottle, clear plastic bag, blue dye, scissors.

- Read a book about jellyfish.

- Tell children you're going to make jellyfish in a bottle.

- Fill the bottle halfway with water. Add blue dye.

- Cut the plastic bag into strips.

- Tie the strips together to form a jellyfish-like shape.

- Push the plastic "jellyfish" into the dyed water.

- Add more water on top of it.

- Leave at least 2 inches (5 centimeters) of air at the top of the bottle.

- Tightly secure the top to the bottle.

GLOSSARY

agenda (uh-JEN-duh) meeting schedule that lists goals and talking points

background check (BAK-ground CHEK) looking into a person's previous experiences

clients (KLYE-uhnts) parents, people who hire babysitters

dues (DOOZ) club membership fees

emergency (ih-MUR-juhn-see) when something dangerous happens like choking, fire, or breathing problems

fees (FEEZ) costs, charges

first aid (FURST AYD) help given to people who hurt themselves before medical help can be provided

minutes (MIN-its) meeting notes

potluck (PAHT-luhk) when people bring food to share with everyone

president (PREZ-ih-duhnt) the leader

recommend (rek-uh-MEND) to support and promote services

references (REF-ur-uhns-iz) people who can be asked about your past performance in a job

roll call (ROHL KAWL) taking attendance

secretary (SEK-rih-ter-ee) person who takes care of minutes and other paperwork

treasurer (TREZH-ur-ur) person who takes care of money

vice president (VISE PREZ-ih-duhnt) the second person in charge; takes over for president if he/she can't perform duties

INDEX

LEARN MORE

BOOKS

Brown, Harriet. *A Smart Girl's Guide to Babysitting: The Care and Keeping of Kids.* Middleton, WI: American Girl, 2014.

Smith, Molly. *Babysitting Secrets: Everything You Need to Have a Successful Babysitting Business: A Book, Activity Cards, Business Cards, Stickers, and More!* San Francisco: Chronicle Books, 2012.

WEB SITES

International Nanny Association: www.nanny.org

PBS Kids—"Babysitting: The Business": http://pbskids.org/itsmylife/money/babysitting/article7.html

WikiHow—"How to Start Your Own Babysitting Business": www.wikihow.com/Start-Your-Own-Babysitting-Business